Soccer

Kirk Bizley

Heinemann Library
Chicago, Illinois

Customer Service 888-454-2279

Designed by Ken Vail Graphic Design
Illustrations by Graham-Cameron Illustration (Tony O'Donnell)
Printed by Wing King Tong in Hong Kong

04 03 02 01 00
10 9 8 7 6 5 4 3 2 1

Library of Congress Cataloging in Publication Data
Bizley, Kirk.
  Soccer / Kirk Bizley.
    p. cm. – (You can do it!)
  Includes index.
  Summary: An introduction to soccer, describing equipment and moves, with tips on safety, warmups, and cooldowns.
   ISBN 1-57572-962-8 (lib. bdg.)
   1. Soccer for children Juvenile literature. [1. Soccer.]
  I. Title. II. Series: You can do it! (Des Plaines, Ill.)
  GV944.2.B59 1999
  796.334'0973—dc21   99-22661
                                         CIP

Acknowledgments
The author would like to thank the staff and students of Shepton Mallett Community Infants School.

The Publishers would like to thank the following for permission to reproduce photographs:
Allsport/Shaun Botterill, page 20 (bottom); Gareth Boden, page 6 (bottom); Trevor Clifford pages 4, 5, 8, 10, 11, 12, 13, 14, 16, 17, 20 (top); Empics/Matthew Ashton, page 6 (top) 18.

Cover photograph reproduced with permission of Tony Stone Images /Lori Adamski Peck.

Every effort has been made to contact copyright holders of any material reproduced in this book. Any omissions will be rectified in subsequent printings if notice is given to the publisher.

To Jake

Some words are shown in bold, **like this.** You can find out what they mean by looking in the Glossary.

Contents

What Do You Need? 4

Where Do You Play? 6

Are You Ready? 8

Shall We Start? 10

Can You Kick? 12

Can You Pass? 14

Can You Dribble? 16

Let's Try Shooting 18

Use Your Head 20

Playing Safe 22

Glossary 24

More Books to Read 24

Index .24

What Do You Need?

To play soccer, you might wear a uniform of a **jersey** or T-shirt, shorts, knee socks, and soccer shoes.

Shin guards are worn inside your socks. They protect your legs from being kicked.

SAFETY STAR
You should wear shin guards when playing or practicing soccer.

In cold weather, you might wear a sweatshirt or warm-up jacket and pants.

If you are playing outside on grass, wear soccer shoes. The **cleats** help your feet get a grip so that you do not slip.

Soccer balls are plastic or leather. You can get them in different sizes. A smaller ball is probably best for you.

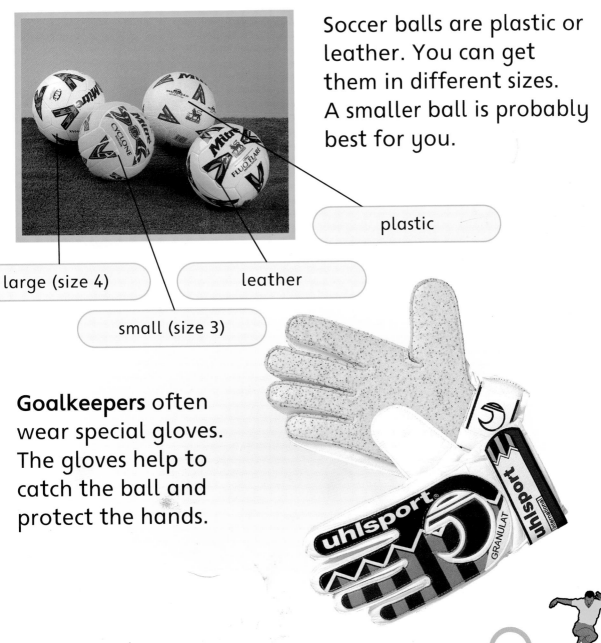

plastic

large (size 4)

leather

small (size 3)

Goalkeepers often wear special gloves. The gloves help to catch the ball and protect the hands.

Where Do You Play?

There are many places to play soccer, but you should never play near a road!

You can play outside. . .

or you can play inside, in a gym or an indoor arena.

Any safe, open space is good for playing soccer. A nearby park is a good place to play, too.

SAFETY STAR
Be sure that it's OK to play soccer in the place you have chosen.

This is what a grass soccer field looks like.
This is the best place to play.

It is divided up by white lines. It has the
correct goal areas, too.

Are You Ready?

Before you play soccer, make sure your body is ready. This is called a **warm-up**. It helps you to play better and keeps you from hurting yourself.

Start with a short run, perhaps around a soccer field.
You can even **dribble** a ball around with you.

SAFETY STAR
Do warm-up exercises before each soccer practice or game.

Now you need to get your muscles warmed up. Getting your muscles warm and stretchy will help you to move easily. Try these **stretching** exercises.

➤Calf Stretch
This stretches the lower muscles in your legs.

▼Quadriceps Stretch
This stretches the big muscles at the top front part of your legs.

▲Hamstring and Lower Back Stretch
This stretches the top-back part of your legs, and your lower back.

Shall We Start?

One way of getting used to a soccer ball is to practice catching and throwing it.

Start by rolling the ball along the ground.

Practice with a partner. Roll the ball to each other. Try picking the ball up in two hands as it comes to you.

Goalkeepers are the only players who are allowed to use their hands in a soccer game while the ball is in play.

Now try a **throw**-in.
Use two hands.
Snap your body
forward as you
throw the ball from
above your head.

You can practice
throw-ins with a
partner. You can
even practice
goalkeepers'
catches when the
ball is thrown.

You can make the throws a bit different
by throwing down. This makes the ball
bounce before it gets to your partner.

Can You Kick?

Learn to kick the ball correctly so you don't hurt your foot. For short kicks and passes, kick with the inside of your foot. Never kick with your toes!

keep your eyes on the ball

use the inside of your foot

follow through with your foot

Begin by putting the ball next to your foot. Make sure the ball is not moving before you kick it. Try kicking the ball with your left foot and your right foot.

For fun, try kicking at targets. Cones make good targets. See if you can hit them with the ball.

Have a partner roll the ball to you. Try using your foot to stop the ball. Make sure you are lined up with the ball as it comes to you.

When you can stop the ball, you have learned to **trap** the ball. Trapping the ball makes the ball easier to kick away.

STAR TIP

Ball control is very important. Remember, you won't be able to use your hands in a real game.

Can You Pass?

Passing means kicking the ball to someone else.
In a game, you pass the ball to your teammates.

To pass, you need to practice controlling the ball.
You need to be able to kick it just where you want.

Practice passing with a partner. Start close to each other. Don't move further apart until you can **trap** and pass the ball every time.

To practice on your own, all you need is a ball and a wall.

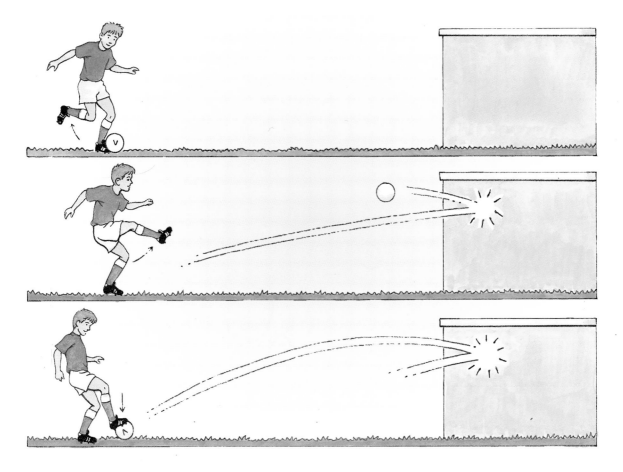

Try passing the ball a long way with a partner. You might need to get the ball up and off the ground. You can do this by leaning back and getting your foot underneath the ball.

Can You Dribble?

Dribbling means moving the ball along the ground with your feet and controlling it all the time.

You can use the front, the inside, the outside, the back, or even the bottom of your foot!

One of the great things about dribbling is that you can practice by yourself.

STAR TIP

When you are learning to dribble, don't go too fast. Start by walking. Then go a little faster.

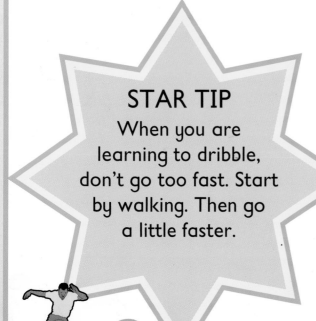

When you practice, try going forward, backward, and sideways. Use all the parts of your foot and practice using both feet.

Set up a course to dribble around. Cones are good to mark a course, but stones or clothing work well, too.

Dribbling is one of the most important moves in soccer. It takes a lot of practice. You need to watch where you are going and to dribble around things at the same time.

Let's Try Shooting

To score a goal you have to **shoot**! Shooting is like making a fast **pass**. You have to get the ball into the other team's goal, or net, without the **goalkeeper** stopping it.

Kick the ball hard when you shoot and get it between the goal posts. Practice kicking the ball into different parts of an empty goal.

Remember, practice using both feet.

STAR TIP
Being on target is more important than kicking hard!

It is fun to practice shooting the ball with friends. This is also a chance to practice other soccer skills. You can pass the ball to each other before you shoot. You can take turns being the goalkeeper.

If there are enough players, you can have a soccer game. Keep score and see which team wins.

Use Your Head

You are allowed to use your head for **heading** the ball. But you must be very careful not to hurt yourself when you do a header.

It is a good idea to start with a balloon or a beach ball.

Remember these rules when you are heading. They should help to keep you from getting hurt.

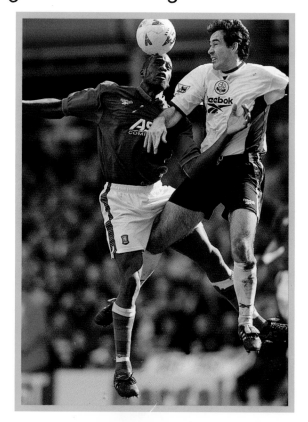

1 Only use your forehead. That is the area just above your eyes and below your hairline.

2 Get underneath and in line with the ball.

3 Always keep your eyes open. Watch the ball all the time.

Once you can head a very soft ball, you can start to use an indoor ball. Later, try with a plastic ball.

You can practice headers by yourself. Toss the ball in front of you, then head it back into the air and catch it.

Try practicing with a partner. Gently toss the ball to each other and try to head it back. Remember, do this first with light, soft balls.

When you get very good at heading forward, you may be able to head backward, too.

Playing Safe

Rules

These are some of the basic rules of soccer.

1. Never use your hands to control the ball while it is in play. Only the **goalkeeper** is allowed to do this.

2. Only **tackle** someone if they have the ball.

3. Don't tackle the goalkeeper.

4. The ball should stay inside the lines of the soccer field during a game.

5. Have an adult in charge make sure everyone plays the game by the rules.

6. Wear **shin guards** to protect your legs.

7. Don't lift your feet too high when you kick, especially if there are others near you.

8. Don't play in dangerous places. Never play near a road.

9. Only kick the ball. Be careful not to kick the other players.

10. The adults in charge make the decisions. Don't argue with them.

Safety

The adult in charge should check the equipment you use. If you see anything wrong, tell the adult.

Equipment should only be moved by the adults.

Make sure you are dressed correctly for soccer. If you have shoes with **cleats**, be sure the cleats are not sharp.

Do **warm-up** exercises to get ready to practice or to play.

Cool-down

When you have finished practicing or playing a game, you should **cool down**. This lets your body get back to normal after all the work it has done.

A simple cool-down is to do all the things you did in your warm-up. Do fewer of the warm-up exercises for a shorter time.

If you do all these things, you will enjoy yourself and be safe. Remember,

YOU CAN DO IT!

Glossary

ball control controlling the ball with any part of your body

cleats rubber or plastic spikes on the bottom of soccer shoes to give extra grip on grass fields

cool-down exercises you do after a workout to relax and cool your body

dribble to move the ball along the ground using your feet

goalkeeper player who stays in the goal, stops goals from being scored; the only player allowed to use his or her hands

heading using your forehead to hit the ball

jersey shirt

pass to send the soccer ball to another player using a kick or header

shin guard pad that fits inside the socks to protect the front of your legs

shoot to aim a kick or header at a goal to try to score

stretching moving your muscles at the joints as far as they will go

tackle to take the ball away from another player

throw-in throwing the ball back onto the field after it has gone outside the white lines during a game

trap to stop the ball by using your feet

warm-up exercises that get your body ready before practicing or playing a game

Index

dribbling 16–17
exercises 8–9, 23
heading 20–21
kicking 12–13
passing 14–15, 18–19
scoring 18–19
soccer field 6–7
rules 10, 22
throw-in 11
trapping 13
uniform 4–5

More Books to Read

Joseph, Paul. *Soccer*. Minneapolis, Minn.: ABDO Publishing Company, 1996.

Palmer, Edward. *Getting Started Sports Books: Soccer*. Westerville, Ohio: Nuway Products, 1997.